there is so much
I want to tell you

there is so much I want to tell you

a Corazón Collective Anthology

Carmen Calatayud
jo reyes-boitel
Angelina Sáenz
ire'ne lara silva
Jen Yáñez-Alaniz

Acknowledgments:

"Godmother" published in *Anti-Heroin Chic,* December 2021
"Hunger Dream" published in *Rogue Agent,* July 2023
"Water Bottles at the Border" published in *IMANIMAN: Poets Writing in the Anzaldúan Borderlands*
"Low Rumble" published in *In the Company of Spirits*
"hot house flower" published in *OyeDrum Magazine*
"we think this world is ours" published in *mouth*
"body" published in *Chachalaca Review*

there is so much i want to tell you

Mouthfeel Press is an indie press publishing works in English and Spanish by
new and established poets and writers. We publish poetry, fiction,
and non-fiction.

Cover Art: "Rómpeme las costillas y acaricia mi corazón"
Nepantlarte Series, 2022, by Octavio Quintanilla
Cover Design: Cloud Cardona
Interior Design: Kimberly James

Contact Information:
Mouthfeelbooks.com
Info.mouthfeelbooks@gmail.com

ISBN: 978-1-957840-28-4

Published in the United States, 2024

First Printing in English
$16

contents

Carmen Calatayud

Godmother

There's a woman on her front porch
Inhaling her cigarette. She's in love

With the slender white stick
Between her fingers.

My fingers pretend to play piano
While tapping my left arm.

Blue-green vein rises and
I stroke it like a purring cat.

It's been four weeks, heroin,
And I need you to feel nothing.

There is so much I want to tell you—
I want to thank you for being my godmother.

For taking me to the church where god doesn't care
And we don't pretend he does.

Truth blooms in a way a moon girl can understand
Truth being there is no me.

Just velvet junk afterglow that
Streams from stars into my arm.

On the sidewalk in front of my feet
A gray feather just landed.

The woman lights another cigarette
The smoke smells like her name, Dulce.

I pick up the feather and put its point
To my vein, dream of burnt caramel

Streaming in, lips smack from fast joy—
The sweet blur gone too quick.

Wish alchemy alone could blow my heart open
Fill it with lips to kiss all the losses

Kill the desire for godmother's hug.

Hunger Dream

Comunidad Valenciana, España (1939-1942)

This violet sky rains almonds.
I try to catch one on my tongue.
The rest drop to the ground and
We gather them in sacks for sustenance.
Our dreams brown almonds.
Our eyes brown almonds.
We stop to break open a few and
Eat together. We kneel because our
Ancestors gave love to these native trees.
The tree limbs grew to the clouds, and
The clouds released almonds.
We smuggle almonds in aprons and pants.
The wind is hungry so we feed it almonds.
We labyrinth our way home with
Hope that flies inside our skulls.
Our DNA sings under the sun.
Today we don't taste blue emptiness.
We taste bark, branch and shell.
For tonight we are stripped of wild twilight fear.

Water Bottles at the Border

After photograph by Delilah Montoya,
Desire Lines, Baboquivari Peak, AZ
2004, printed 2008, ink-jet print

I.

Dream: A saint with a white guayabera
Unloads jugs to dot the desert,
Water to ease swelling tongues.

2.

He walks for wandering people,
Leaves bottles for thirsty women
In this burnt coral sunset land:
Two countries so close the border
Evaporates at night.

3.

Filled plastic jugs hidden behind
Jumping cholla in this vista of hope.

4.

Awake: The monsters of fire will come
For you, gun you down under
A moon of ginger flames,
Just as your whispers begin to rise.

5.

This borderland named many times,
Stolen and taken back again.
The saguaros refuse to fight,
Stretch into glitter-blue sky as
White heat feeds the ground.

6.
We chant for survival.
Ravens fly overhead,
Offer ebony rings of faith.

7.
If no one knows us
Our bones will mingle
With this dry earth.
They will hiss our names
In the wind.

Tentative Love in the Time of Insomnia

This might be a sleepless love poem
about wandering where orange blossom scent
bleeds into air like a cut on the wrist that won't clot

This might be a sleepless love poem
about melodic ghosts who leave copper stains
on the floor and song lyrics inside walls

This might be a sleepless love poem
about resurrection between legs,
flesh that remembers satellite touch and
steam that comes from a stray exhale

This might be a sleepless love poem
about my nostalgic heart and your monstrous hands
that were once an x-ray of improbable bones

This might be a sleepless love poem
about how we can't find angels or Jupiter's
trail, but we take a corner of the sky—
a part of it that goes unnoticed and still hums.

Low Rumble

For Michael Hughes, 1959-2011

There's no hiding from your empty bed.
Your carcass is gone.
Your spirit airlifted by the last chopper.

Across the way, a doctor tries to siphon gas
from your brain. He prays to your body
for answers as he writes the autopsy report,
his science no match for the machinations
you morphed into rocket man art.

Sell the watch. Sell the clocks.
I don't care what time it is
anymore. Your heavenly destination
waits but I refuse to mail your dust.
It's been weeks since you made
your way out of this world.
I bet you're sitting in Emerald City
with a frozen drink in your hand,
telling jokes to the Wicked Witch.
You know I kept hoping you would
choose the right pills and pop them
at the appropriate times.

Big flyaway moon, that's you.
Pieces of comet tail trail off after
you're gone. Chunks of stars
break and I imagine them
chasing you through the sky.

In another world, the helicopter that carries
your spirit lands next to the pyramids.
A thousand camels cross the sands.
Their low rumble reminds me of you.

jo reyes-boitel

body[1]
[definition]
noun \ bä-dē \

Related to Old High German *botah* from the 9th century, but of unknown origin.
Replaced in use by *Leib*, originally "life," and *Körper*, from Latin.

I.   the sense or idea of something that takes space or has purpose.
every cell with its purpose, every breath its own world.
What cannot be undone.

2a.   the trunk — the truth — without its limbs to tell an opposing story.
my hands say yes but my core shows I will not budge.
or, matter, a beauty in symmetry – set adrift in an ocean
without boundary, no stars for guidance – tethered
to the magnet stirring within this earth.
The truth of the matter [a saying].

2b.   the heart, viscous, constant.
the density of this house, how walking away
doesn't equal escape.

3.   a mass, distinct from another mass.
water, the tension holding all just at the lip of a glass.
sana sana colita de rana [colloquial].

4a.   the enclosed portion; a secret. also, a portion of text. a dress,
cloaking the figure.
my shoulders shrouded in misplaced history.

4b.   sound box. reverberations along the walls used to define
the dimensions of the matter.
my ear against your chest reveals the ocean's entirety.

5.   community: a group of linked people.
to be strong is to ask to have that strength tested.

---

1 Some definitions pulled and reworked from Merriam-Webster Dictionary online and origin of the word notes are from Online Etymology Dictionary.

6a. fullness. rich. the weight of a sip of wine. the blood
     circulating. release. new life.
     this is me. this is my body. this. touch this.
     ocean floor, mushroom cap, tilled soil.
     tree rings, sandstone, mold.
     dust. wind.
     eggshell.

6b. resonance.
     hum.

See also, *fallacy* or *hymnal.*

chrysanthemum

elegy for Gloria Anzaldúa

tell me the truth   the world has ended in a burst
petals blown away from
a flower's nearly imperceptible eye

                filmy scales,
fish's skin flecking along billowed cheeks
                  like stars unraveling,
condensed, churning from center to surface

          dark matter
heavy iron molten   mirrored hematite
then cooling mica iridescent and

                            falling away
into translucent sheets   purples and greens rain down
oceanic salt living in these bodies

      they say
we are built of stardust

                I want to believe
some part of us took a breath before we were this,
and that this breath continues after us
              I want to believe
           you are here | have left | will return

        not enough
to say you were beautiful
in those dark rooms
       I dream you in softness: slip shoes, ivory silk,
and a forest green sweater, its large collar
framing your heart-shaped face
I feel like an intruder to your nighttime sky,
watching you while you choose your bracelets,

turn your palms back and forth — they are song birds
in the air, light surrounding you   you
watch my eyes follow you

                                then pull
                                at still warm amber
        until it glistens
and promise to embrace me within its walls

I kiss your palms, find pearls and yellow gold

hot house flower

it is a dream without a start   rooted by our mothers, tied
to the eggs we must carry   a wish rubbed into foreheads
with sweet almond oil while we sleep

sugar
sugared flesh
creamed petals of papercuts

                         the person at home has become a stranger
I sit in my car a few blocks away   parked
lights off   the radio low   I debate my tiredness
                         things are not going well

I'm told compromise is a loving act   I resist
    ounce by ounce I feel the loss
Love is a building up   they say   a fulfillment   a joy

        like weddings how girls long for them
        tender fleshed
                shaded in perfume
fists of peonies portend happy marriages

this life we are made to hope for   ((collective exhale))
    cake   marked calendars   gorgeous flowers

in good soil peonies live a hundred years   planted once
they circle back each spring   claim their land again
in anniversary

((I'll try to make this clear:
I'm lost.))

I saw you weeks ago on the street
after years of not   you were just far enough
from the bar's entrance   noncommittal
        cordiality is the art of denial

we first met in the 2nd floor hallway of a small apartment
neighbors bribed with beer to allow the racket
of a sometime band
        behind the drum set   sticks in hand
        triggered foot tapping
                    you

later we sat   arm leaning on arm   avoiding eyes
the clank of a pool table falling away

you walked me home through the soaked streets
it was there   a block away   you pushed me against the fence
your face my face wet breath   heat radiating
from the sidewalk   in the dead of August
your hands   pulling at my doubt

((I've been told I use this mouth
for more than what it's good for))

this was years ago

now
        by chance   I have found you

I say aloud   *I'm going home*
me in my lavender coat leaving all my friends

        turning the corner of the blues bar
you have followed me   we pretend
you are a stranger   you   who should be home
child and wife intoxicated by sleep

shoulders in a rush   your grip as unforgiveable
as I remember
I stumble   my cold lips fall into your neck
                a kind of hot house embrace

this is where I will tell myself
the moment overtook me   I wasn't thinking
    clearly   I'd had one too many drinks

but the truth is I wanted out of the facade
wanted to self-destruct and take everything with me

        which requires a plan

and so I arranged for this   ((all along))
since your name rose during conversation
with a shared friend

I planned to watch you play those drums again
your shirt off in the overheated bar

planned to have you watch me   walk out
        you   not knowing what you were capable of
but following still
        anything to undo the life assumed for me
anything to not follow this destruction alone
because I don't know any other way out
and my house is sleeping
        in the darkness of the longest night of the year

your health and safety at Oedipus Rex + Lilacs

Sometimes you need only to hear where someone was born
to understand they have sorrow swimming through their body.

Take Igor Stravinsky, of Russia, who birthed controversy
with The Rite of Spring. That, with its sharp notes
and angled dancers' bodies, nearly started a riot.

Or, George Walker, Washington DC-born, taught piano
by black women in a space that did not want his art
or his music because they were born from
black limbs, a black mind.

And music can be conjecture and ambiguity and
redefined by circumstance — a design enabling the listener
to return to its score later, to pretend
they have always understood.

But the words in this music — those suffer
the chance of misunderstanding, often
to the detriment of the writer.

So enter the librettists: Jean Cocteau,
speaking of cursed gods, or Walt Whitman,
in love with Lincoln, in love with this country's potential,
while also holding its broken heart.

Opened curtains become a kind of dark fate.
          your health is our priority
                    we are eager to welcome you back

  but there are many concerns

The instruments' whining becomes a meditation on grief.
          Be assured:

          top priority
                    safety measures

proof of vaccine requirement
mask enforcement
health ventilation initiative
increased cleaning & sanitation

Each musician stands in for remembrance.
join us
feel confident   *reach out*

* Title pulled from Opera Philadelphia email regarding safety of in-person attendees for upcoming performance. Partial found poem lines from that email's text.

we think this world is ours

I go straight from work to a benefit party. The invited
are asked to arrive in *vintage queer thrift store realness*.
I am not prepared, but there is a vendor and I walk through
with an 80s old man tie — yellow and blue striped wide
bottomed satiny polyester.
I'm a travesty but my lipstick is on point.

It is a catwalk through the gallery, to the raffle table,
and into the backyard for a seat at the drag show.
The kings have sensible shoes but the queens are struggling
with their heels in the moist soil.

There are so many here and I don't think I know any of them.
    Young queers.
It's a Tuesday and my friends, coupled at home
and making dinner, recount their workdays in the comfort
of a television's glow.
                                        I am relieved
and thankful when one of the queens adjusts my tie,
kisses me on the cheek. It is a kindness.

It could sustain me for weeks.

Plants prepare themselves for dormancy.
They have learned to not depend on us.
    Blooms are a signal of urgency,
a desperate hope
their story will continue
despite the approaching cold.

At home, someone who is no longer a lover, never a friend,
sits on the couch, contemplating our chances.
Doe eyes look up when I unlock the door.
They want to know but will not ask
why I've come back so late,
and with an ill-knotted tie
and shimmer on my face.

Pain will not fade, it will insist on its desperate call.
We will cut at the beauty of this dying thing,
hold its arrangement of last breaths and

      without reason,
something within us
will admire the other's attempt
to blossom.

Angelina Sáenz

On the postcard of Monumento Cervantes

taped to my kitchen cabinet
you can see my lover's window
there on the 19th floor
of the Torre de Madrid building
that towers behind the statue of
Don Quixote and Sancho Panza

Count to 19

Allí está el

Books we left at each other's house

always the reason we'd get back together

I know it's over
because you haven't called looking for your books
and I haven't called looking for mine

Did you order another copy of Darwish?

I still haven't replaced Neruda

You tore my dress

when you undressed me
between kisses and thrusts

and then

you sewed the strap back on
while I was sleeping

You are not the boss of me

but I am, Angelina

I am the boss of you

Es que todavía no te das cuenta

Your tongue

is a warm, Caribbean wave

rolling on my clit

iréne lara silva

corazón espinado

nopal

love all thethorned things with me as Nature made
them thorned and bright and dangerous   not tamed
not domesticated not bred for softness   wild things
require respect   beautiful things should require
careful handling   there is nothing more meaningful
than to be entrusted with the soul of a thing
i can't remember if it was my vision or my brother's
but i carry the image in my heart   all golden
and green   radiant and radiant and radiant   paint god in
the shape of nopales   make the canvas hold the
reflection of the sun   make it so that our eyes can't
see all of it at once   so that our eyes can't rest on it
because the face of god would drive us mad
love all the thorned things with me because life is
beautiful and terrible   because everything alive
carries its death   because nopales never surrender
never cease their rebirthings   because we live like
this   creating fiercely   fierce thorned creatures
carrying our deaths and carrying our medicine

ocotillo

i loved to learn ocotillos by loving them small
bound by small containers watching their rounded
leaves grow alongside their thorns
oh but what i feel when i see them growing wild i
greeted the first one i saw on I-10 as if it was a long
lost relative as if it was the first sign of returning
home as if it rooted in solid rock and perched
against the sun and the sky knew my name
how can i truly be alone if the ocotillos are there
thorned and bare or leafing or blooming
when i die i want to go back to being a part of the
wind i'm tired of being human and being human
and being human but if it isn't time yet then let me
join the ocotillos let my eyes thorn and my hands
thorn and my voice thorn may my soul entirely
thorn over

cholla

we called them 'botanical samples'   not 'cuttings'
we never asked people or plant nurseries for
permission   if the pieces were there to be
collected   or if the plant itself was willing to
have a part of itself 'liberated'

            there was an entire season when my brother was
        mad for chollas   there was one we eyed on the
          corner of south first street   another growing in a
                cadillac turned botanical public art behind the
                                                        planet k

botanical samples in my bag   in my pocket   in a
water bottle   in a ziploc   in a paper bag
in a moistened paper towel

            do you know how difficult it is to carry thorned
                        things in secret

before that season of collecting   of watching
him with tweezers and tongs and absolute
concentration   i wouldn't have been able to
tell you what a cholla was

now every cholla tells me its name   i saw them
            blooming in new mexico in the snow only a few
            weeks after his first birthday in the other world
                    is grief a thorn or is it a flower

maguey

Grabé en la penca de un maguey tu nombre
unido al mío/ entrelazados/ como una prueba ante/
la ley del monte/ que ahí estuvimos/ enamorados
– José Ángel Espinosa Aragón, "La Ley del Monte"

there's a taquería on Riverside that's open late and
that makes a queso flameado you can add chorizo
and nopales and mushrooms too   i love their
tiny tacos bistek with sautéed onions and cilantro
and lime juice   i love taking their large
frijoles a la charra bowl and divvying it up into
smaller bowls   the secret is to do it quickly
mercilessly without fear   i've spent many late
nights there and plan to spend many more
but what makes me pause every time i go there is
the maguey   wide and sharp edged   like a
bouquet of green machetes   only feet from the
front door   it's alive but scarred   layers and
layers of graffiti   names and initials   and
yes   messages and hearts and arrows and i
wonder if the ones who carved into the maguey
knew the song
what you vow to the maguey   cannot be
betrayed   the maguey will not be lied to
the penalty is your blood your life your entire story
this is the law of the monte of the wilderness of
nature of thorned or sharp edged things
my heart is scarred and written over but it was born
in the monte   it lives and dreams in the
monte   it is more monte than human more animal
than human   proceed carefully   time has not
made it surrender its sharpness

*from "La Ley del Monte" by Jose Angel Espinosa Aragon

crown of thorns

when i was a child there was a bougainvillea in
front of my mother's house   it bloomed year round
and it was always green   fifty years and i've
never seen another bougainvillea with a trunk as
wide as that one   its branches cascaded over
when i was small i could crawl inside and lie on the
earth   shaded from the sun   and if the thorns
pricked me   if they scratched my skin or sipped at
my blood   i never cried never became
upset   i understood i was paying the price
for not being careful enough

years ago   when the snow came   my brother
and i lost eleven bougainvilleas   red
golden   white pink   every color you could
think of   they were huge   taller than i
was   and as the days passed without power or
heat or running water i didn't think to try to do
anything else to try to save them   and so
they were all lost   and i had to cut them up and
uproot them and say farewell to their dry husks
even though their spirits were long gone

i thought we would try again and we did   and
bougainvilleas bloomed outside our window again
and then my brother was gone   and in my
grief i found home for the new bougainvilleas there
are three left   all small   different colors
i thought about trying to rebuild them again
i still love bougainvilleas more than any other
blooming thing   but these last three seem to be
pining for another home

meanwhile the four crown of thorns are outgrowing
their pots   blooming white and yellow
and red and pink   as if the excessive sun and
record breaking heat just makes them laugh
i water them when i can   they don't droop
they don't complain   the wind knocks them down
they lose earth   they don't seem to care
i pick them up and their leaves are still a luxurious
green and their blooms are intact

i love stubborn things   in a few days i'll
repot them   they need bigger pots so that the
wind won't have its way with them so often and i
won't be able to touch them   i'll have to use silicon
gloves and tongs and some twine   a not small
amount of cursing will also be required   and i
might shed some blood or gain new scars   but
what love doesn't require some sacrifice

Jen Yáñez-Alaniz

Muse

I get close enough for you
to touch my dress,

the lavender hue of cotton.
I witness the birds fuss,

swoop & squawk,
satisfied to hover.

Those birds they peck,
their beaks they take of your

flesh, devour verses
meant for me,

The Magdalene standing by
wanting.

My lids & limbs heavy,
feeling the need growing,

carefully I merely skim
your skin,

the smooth tone, strength
honed by verse & vigor,

the stirring from under
your soft cotton shirt.

I, an aging woman
desperate,

strain & ache
in the ovaries,

tightness in the uterus,
breast tender

with a need to nourish,
my body wanting to receive

—into that space
where motherhood is born.

The Magdalene
from within me escapes.

I am left to hold the host,
to sip the wine.

I leave you at the tomb.

Autumn

Stems curve, sprawling
& revealing

an intimate bud. It's a rosy thing,
it moistens as she anticipates

October's brisk morning.
Delirious & dumb, nocturnal creatures spin.

Emerald moths take in sweet nectar & drift
into the haze of harvest's moon as it wanes.

In my dream of flowering & fireflies,
October comes to me as a bird, its soft wings,

the azure warmth of Texas skies.
Clamped in its beak, soft pods dangle.

My tongue unravels to touch the furred
surface of fruit

yearning to be born.

Senescence

Texas daisies
paint roadsides vibrant yellow

Fragrance expands
the scent exposes earth

& her aromatic decay
shaped by primal bone of shale

by fallen branches & erosion
revealing sparrows in their most

tender state of seek & flight
for faded stem & ambered blade

to build its home
to build its home

This trampled petal that I am
below branches & erosion
yet needs to be desired

This injured petal that I am
below branches & erosion
wants sparrow's tenderness

of seek & flight
that the sparrow

might take me home
might take me home

to nestle
in the splendor
of its toil

Time

it exists
in a sky above my home

on one
October night

when I didn't step outside
to look

yo sé
que en esas horas
las nubes iluminadas
exhalaban

Imagino mi hogar
como una madre
dormida

como una iglesia
agotada

cansada del matrimonio

unraveling herself
from sterling light

unraveling herself

from the moon

I believe in the promise

that you'll arrive as autumn's
first dusk settles, as the pink air
dissolves into darkness.

I believe that if I shield
myself from anxious summer
rays as I await you, the sky
will thin into tomorrow
— one day closer.

I believe that you and I
will never be eternal lovers,

no cambiaremos
para amarnos con pasión.

Creo que mientras tanto lo espero,
in its rosy feverish glow,

— autumn's tempered light
will never reach us.

Authors' Biographies

Carmen Calatayud is the daughter of immigrants: A Spanish father and Irish mother. Her book *In the Company of Spirits* (2012) was a runner-up for the Academy of American Poets Walt Whitman Award and a finalist for the Andrés Montoya Poetry Prize. Her work has appeared in journals such as *Cutthroat, Poet Lore, Rogue Agent, Tahoma Literary Journal* and *Verse Daily*, and several anthologies. Carmen is a Larry Neal Poetry Award winner and a Virginia Center for the Creative Arts fellow.

jo reyes-boitel is a queer, mixed Latinx poet, playwright, and scholar. Completing their MFA at the University of Texas–Rio Grande Valley, jo is a Presidential Research Fellow and teaches undergraduate creative writing courses. jo's work centers on decoloniality and the role of longing and mourning in reclamation. Publications include *Michael + Josephine* (FlowerSong Press, 2019), *mouth* (Neon Hemlock, 2021), and *the matchstick litanies* (Next Page Press, 2023). Recent publications include *Zócalo Public Square, Huizache Magazine,* and *Acentos Review.*

Angelina Sáenz is an award-winning educator and poet. She is a UCLA Writing Project fellow, an alumna of the VONA/Voices Workshop for Writers of Color and a Macondo Writer's Workshop Fellow. Her poetry has appeared in *Diálogo, Split this Rock, Out of Anonymity, Angels Flight Literary West, Every Other, Cockpit Revue Paris* and *The Acentos Review.* She has two books of poetry, Edgecliff (FlowerSong Press, 2021) and *Maestra* (FlowerSong Press, 2023).

ire'ne lara silva, the 2023 Texas State Poet Laureate, is the author of five poetry collections, *the eaters of flowers, furia, Blood Sugar Canto, CUICACALLI/House of Song,* and *FirstPoems,* and a short story collection, *flesh to bone,* which won the Premio Aztlán. ire'ne is currently a Writer at Large for *Texas Highways Magazine* and is working on a second collection of short stories titled, *the light of your body.* Her first comic book, *VENDAVAL,* will be released by the Chispa Imprint of Scout Comics in April 2024. http://www.irenelarasilva.wordpress.com

Jen Yáñez-Alaniz is a Chicana Mestiza activist, educator, and poet. She is a PhD Fellow in Culture, Literacy, and Language at the University of Texas, San Antonio. As co-founder of *Welcome: A Poetry Declaration*, she brings awareness through equity-driven conversations centered on the preservation of language and language literacy. Her work, *Matrilineal Poetics: Toward an Understanding of Corporeality and Identity* is featured in Latinas in Hollywood Herstories. Her poetry is published in various journals and anthologies including an extensive critical biography of Carmen Tafolla in *Chicana Portraits,* edited by Dr. Norma E. Cantú. She is the author of *Surrogate Eater* (Alabrava Press, 2023).